TENTS, TIGERS AND THE RINGLING BROTHERS

Badger Biographies

Other Badger Biographies

Mai Ya's Long Journey

A Recipe for Success: Lizzie Kander and Her Cookbook

TENTS, TIGERS AND THE RINGLING BROTHERS

by Jerry Apps

Wisconsin Historical Society Press

Published by the Wisconsin Historical Society Press

www.wisconsinhistory.org

All images are courtesy of the Wisconsin Historical Society's Circus World Museum unless otherwise indicated.

Photographs identified with PH, WHi, or WHS are from the Society's collections; address inquiries about such photos to the Visual Materials Archivist at the above address.

Printed in the United States of America
Cover design by Nancy Zucker

11 10 09 08 07   1 2 3 4 5

Library of Congress Cataloging-in-Publication Data

Apps, Jerold W., 1934–
  Tents, tigers, and the Ringling brothers / by Jerry Apps.
     p. cm.—(Badger biographies)
  Includes bibliographical references and index.
  ISBN-13: 978-0-87020-374-9 (pbk. : alk. paper)
  ISBN-10: 0-87020-374-6 (pbk. : alk. paper)
  1. Ringling Brothers Barnum and Bailey Combined Shows—History—Juvenile literature. 2. Ringling Brothers—History—Juvenile literature. 3. Ringling family—Juvenile literature. 4. Wisconsin—Genealogy—Juvenile literature. I. Title.
  GV1821.R5A664 2007
  791.309—dc22

                              2006018006

∞ The paper used in this publication meets the minimum requirements of the American National Standard for Information Sciences—Permanence of Paper for Printed Library Materials, ANSI Z39.48-1992.

Contents

1 The Idea for a Circus 1

2 Putting the Show on the Road 11

3 The First Ringling Big Top 21

4 A Circus on the Rails 32

5 The Circus Comes to Town 37

6 Meet the Ringling Brothers 55

7 The Ringling Menagerie 69

8 Winter Quarters 79

Afterword 89

Appendix 93
  The Ringling Brothers 93
  Ringling Time Line 97

Glossary 100

Reading Group Guide and Activities 104

To Learn More about the Circus 107

Acknowledgments 109

Index 111

1

The Idea for a Circus

The Ringling boys heard the steam whistle of the riverboat before they could see it paddling up the river. The whistle meant visitors were coming to town. Growing up in McGregor, Iowa, on the Mississippi River, the boys had seen many

riverboats. Steam engines powered these huge boats. Some of the boats were 3 or 4 stories tall and 250 feet long.

The hustle and bustle of steam boats on the Mississippi

The town of McGregor, Iowa, sits on the banks of the Mississippi. This photo is from about 1870.

The boats carried supplies and people up and down the great river.

The year was 1869 and McGregor, Iowa, with 2,000 people, was a bustling city. Its location on the Mississippi River made it a stopping point for settlers and others going west. Pioneers crossed the Mississippi River on a ferryboat at McGregor and sometimes stayed several days before moving on. Many of them bought **provisions**, such as flour and salt, in McGregor. Some of them needed repairs for their horse harnesses before they traveled west by horses and covered wagons.

The Ringling family lived in this tiny house in McGregor.

By 1869, there were 7 Ringling boys. At 16, Al was the oldest with Gus just a year younger. Otto was 11, and then followed the 4 youngest brothers: 6-year-old Alf T., 4-year-old Charles, and 3-year-old John. Baby Henry was not even a year old.

provision: supplies of food and drinks

2

August Ringling made leather horse harnesses like the one this horse is wearing.

The oldest 3—Al, Gus, and Otto—helped their father, August Ringling, in his harness-making shop. In the shop, they made leather harnesses for horses, and they also made buggy whips and horse collars. The boys helped by cutting large pieces of leather into narrow strips. Then they sewed these strips of leather together. The strips would become horse harnesses. They also decorated horse-drawn carriages with leather. The days were long and the work was hard.

While their brothers worked, Alf T., Charles, and John played outside the shop and on the streets of McGregor. As soon as they reached 10 years of age, each of them would also work with their father in the shop. Carefree childhood didn't last long!

3

The large Ringling family was very poor. The harness-making business barely provided enough money for the family to put food on the table. Large factories had begun making harnesses. People working in factories with machines could cut and sew leather much more quickly than people could by hand. Thus the Ringling shop, where the boys and their father made harnesses by hand, had a hard time trying to stay in business.

When the Ringling boys heard the steamboat's whistle blow, all but baby Henry hurried to the McGregor boat landing.

Which of these performers do you think the Ringling brothers liked the most?

Many riverboats stopped in McGregor, but one day in 1869 it was a circus boat. A circus riverboat was special. Dan Rice's famous circus that traveled on the Mississippi River had pulled up to shore. The boys watched the crew unload the riverboat's cargo of elephants, other wild animals, performing horses, and equipment. Workmen quickly set up the big circus tent on a vacant lot in town. The tent seated 5,000 people. Families from the area came to see the circus, some traveling many miles by horse and buggy.

Dan Rice's circus had 3 acts going on at the same time: a running horse with a rider carrying a girl on his shoulder, a singer wearing striped pants playing a banjo, and 2 clowns leapfrogging over each other. Visitors to the circus also could see wild animals—tigers, bears, monkeys, alligators, and ostriches—animals that people who lived along the upper Mississippi River had never seen. In 1869, there were very few zoos in the country, no movies, and of course, no television where people could see wild animals from other parts of the world. So the arrival of the circus amazed young and old alike, but especially boys and girls the ages of the Ringlings.

Other riverboat circuses visited McGregor. They traveled from New Orleans, Louisiana, to St. Paul, Minnesota, stopping at the many river towns along the way. Every summer, riverboat circuses stopped in McGregor, set up their big tents, and put on stunning shows.

After seeing the riverboat circuses, the Ringling boys decided to set up their own circus during their free time on the weekends. It was to be a circus *for* kids and performed *by* kids: the Ringling boys to be exact. As the oldest, Al Ringling led the way. His most famous act involved a neighbor's old white horse. Al borrowed the horse and learned to stand up on its back while it pranced in a circle.

RINGLING BROTHERS' FIRST PARADE.

Alf T.'s sketch of the Ringling boy's first circus parade

In the beginning, the Ringlings charged 10 straight pins for admission. The pins were probably used by their mother for sewing—a valuable item in those days. Later, the brothers charged a single penny. Neighbors began calling the Ringling play circus a "penny" circus.

As their penny circus got bigger, the boys began to advertise their show by putting on parades. One after another, they walked down Main Street in McGregor pulling toy wagons that carried some of the "wild" animals that would be in their show—a couple of kittens, some dogs, and several cats. The shows took place in an old barn in their neighborhood. Inside, the boys built several exhibits and made big, homemade signs to identify what they were showing. In one, a gigantic bullfrog sat in a little cage with a sign reading: "From Timbuctoo. Captured at great risk from the depths of a far-away swamp from which no other frog-collector ever emerged alive."

A chicken was in another cage. She laid an egg while the children watched. A small cage contained some English sparrows, with a sign that read: "**Imported** From an

imported: brought into a country from another place or region

Unnamed Pacific Island." The boys had even brought over their mother's yellow canary to the barn. The sign in front of its cage read: "The head of a great **dynasty**."

Of course all of the signs went far beyond the truth. Every one of the animals came right from McGregor! The Ringling boys had heard real circus people **boast** about their exhibits and they thought they should too.

The barn was also the place where the boys performed. The older boys, Al, Gus, and Otto, walked across the high

beam in the barn, 10 feet above the floor. They performed on swings and tried some juggling. They even walked on a rope strung tight between 2 beams in the barn.

WHI IMAGE ID 26306

The Ringling brothers "penny circus" took place inside a barn like this.

dynasty: a powerful kingdom or family that has ruled for a long time   **boast:** to talk proudly about yourself in order to impress people

The Ringling's first children's circus was a great success. They put on several more circuses, much to the delight of the town's children who came to watch. Al was especially interested in juggling and tightrope walking. In 1873, when he was 20, he left his family in McGregor and moved to Brodhead in south central Wisconsin. He worked in a wagon and blacksmith shop. On Saturdays during the hot, dull summer, he strung a rope between 2 tall buildings in Brodhead and walked high above the street from one building to another. People crowded around to see the fearless tightrope walker. They were even more amazed when he carried a small cook stove and cooked an entire meal while balancing on the rope!

Al's talent didn't stop there. He also learned to balance a breaking plow on his chin. Farmers used breaking plows to plow soil that had never been tilled. In 1870, a breaking plow weighed about 70 pounds, and it wasn't easy to handle. People passing by couldn't believe that someone could balance such a heavy object on his chin. But Al Ringling could do it perfectly, much to the amazement of crowds that gathered to watch him perform on Main Street in Brodhead. Al was interested in gaining circus experience. He did these

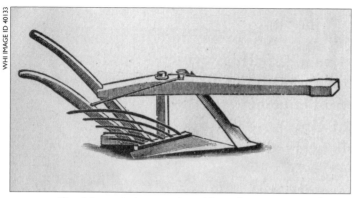

circus tricks without charging money. He did them just because he loved performing and practicing his acts.

Could you balance a breaking plow on your chin like Al Ringling did?

Al and his younger brothers, who had worked side-by-side with their father in his harness shop, wanted to do something different from their father. They wanted to find other work when they became older and started making a living. Al Ringling especially hoped that he might one day have his own circus. But it took money to start a circus, and the only money that Al had was what he had saved from working in Brodhead.

10

2

Putting the Show on the Road

What "fun" and "comic" acts might you see at a Ringling hall show?

To earn enough money to start his own circus, Al came up with the idea of doing hall shows. Hall shows were popular in the late 1800s. A hall show was performed on a stage in a building. The shows usually included music, comedy acts, short plays, and sometimes even dances. The actors and performers moved from town to town by railroad, putting on a show each night. Al knew that he and his brothers and some friends could put on such a show. He set out to get one organized.

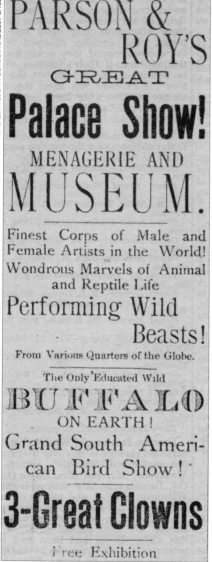

WAUKESHA COUNTY DEMOCRAT, AUGUST 6, 1881

Al Ringling once worked for Parson and Roy's Circus.

In the fall of 1882, when Al was 29, he traveled to Baraboo, Wisconsin, to talk with his father and his brothers about starting a hall show. His father had moved the family to Baraboo in 1875 to open a harness shop.

In 1882, the next younger sons— Gus (now 28) and Otto (now 24)— worked in Minneapolis. The other boys, Alf T., 18, Charles, 17, John, 16, and Henry, 14, lived at home and worked with their father at the shop. By this time, they also had a little sister, Ida, who was 8 years old.

Since 1879, Al Ringling had gained lots of circus experience. He had worked with such circuses as Parson and Roy's Great Palace Show, which had its headquarters in Burlington, Wisconsin.

Al practiced his juggling skills every day and had become quite famous as a juggler. Balancing a breaking plow on his chin was still his favorite juggling act. By this time, John Ringling also had gained some experience working in a circus.

Even though the Ringling family was always poor, their mother had managed to scrape together enough money so her sons could learn to play musical instruments such as the violin and trumpet. By the time Al was ready for a Ringling hall show, Charles was an excellent violinist, and Alf T. had learned to play several instruments, including the trumpet and tuba.

Al told his father and brothers about his plans to organize a hall show where he and his brothers could perform. Al's brothers saw this as an opportunity to leave behind the hard work of making harnesses. They also looked forward to the adventure of traveling from town to town and performing on a stage.

Al planned to use the money he had saved from working in circuses and in wagon shops to get the hall show started. He also hoped the brothers might save enough so they could start their own circus. Al only wanted to do hall shows long enough to earn money to buy a big tent and put a circus on the road.

Their father was not too certain about Al's big dream to do a hall show and then start a circus. But he didn't stand in the way. In 1882, Al Ringling asked Edward Kimball and 3 other actors and musicians from Baraboo to join their **troupe** (troop). Alf T. and Charles would go on the road with them. John Ringling would join them in December. The brothers called their little group of actor-musicians "The Ringling Brothers Classic and Comic Concert Company."

They decided to put on their first show in Mazomanie, Wisconsin, a farming town about 25 miles west of Madison. They chose Mazomanie for their first show because they didn't want their Baraboo friends and neighbors in the audience, making faces and teasing them. The boys loaded

troupe: a group of performers

14

their trunks and musical instruments on horse-drawn wagons and set out for Sauk City (south of Baraboo by a few miles) where they boarded a train for Mazomanie.

The Ringlings held their first hall show on November 27, 1882. They charged 50 cents for adults and 25 cents for children. They had already come a long way from the penny circus! Alf T. later wrote in a book: "We had about a $13 **house**, but the 59 people composing the audience looked bigger (to us) than an audience of 15,000 under our tents does today. It seemed as if every individual knew our history, and was aware that this was our first attempt."

Their goal to keep friends out of the audience failed. Several had followed them to Mazomanie just to see what they were up to. Their **expenses** for the evening, including rental of the hall, totaled $25.90. **Income** from the tickets they sold was only $13.00! They had lost $12.90, which was a lot of money in 1882. It was not a great way to start a business.

house: amount of money made from ticket sales   **expense:** amount of money spent
income: amount of money made from an event or sale

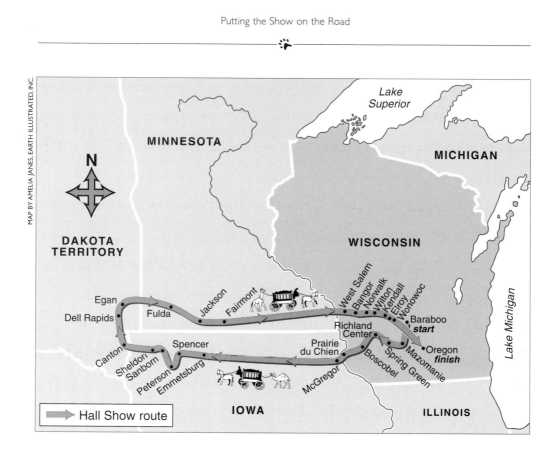

Even with the rough beginning, the Ringlings got back on the train and traveled to the Wisconsin towns of Spring Green, Richland Center, and Boscobel, putting on a show each night. Then they moved on to their hometown of McGregor, Iowa, and then to Prairie du Chien, Wisconsin. John Ringling joined the troupe in Sanborn, Iowa, on December 18. After the first less-than-successful show in Mazomanie, things got better and they gained more experience.

A typical hall show program included an introductory piece performed by all the musicians. Then followed a **cornet** solo, a short play, a violin duet, and a vocal duet sung by Charles and Alf T. Finally, the troupe put on a longer play titled "A Cold Bath, or as Failure a Great Success."

The Ringlings and their troupe continued on. They traveled from small town to small town in Wisconsin, Iowa, the Dakota Territory (which would become the states of North and South Dakota in 1889), and Minnesota. Because they were traveling during the winter, they were often snowed in or snowed out! Most often, they arrived by train. Then from the trains, they traveled by buggy, by horse and sleigh, or on foot. The boys played mostly in little towns in cold, drafty halls. The population of each town was but a few hundred people. An "advance" man, M. A. Young, traveled ahead of the troupe, making arrangements and getting permission to use the halls for their show.

To create excitement for their evening shows, the boys put together parades earlier in the day. The Ringlings marched

cornet: a horn similar to a trumpet, but shorter in length

down the main street of each town. As they marched, they played their instruments and one member beat on a big bass drum. It must have brought back a lot of memories from their first parades in the days of the penny circus!

The Ringling boys put on 107 shows the first winter they were on the road from 1882 to 1883. They did not perform on Sundays, but did work most holidays, including Christmas and New Year's Eve. The first year they didn't make a lot of money, but they did learn how to put on a show that people would pay money to see. They also learned how to put on a show 6 days out of every week, with each show in a different town. That's hard work!

Most importantly, the Ringling boys learned how to work together and get along with each other. They also learned how to get along with people who lived in the small towns of the Midwest. People in small towns were often **suspicious** (sus **pih** shus) of traveling actors. Many traveling stage shows were run by dishonest people, or weren't meant for the whole family. The Ringlings had to

suspicious: mistrustful or fearful of something or someone

18

TO·NIGHT!

RINGLING BROS.'

=== G R A N D ===

CARNIVAL OF FUN!

FUN! FUN! FUN!

The Funniest and Most Refined Show Party on the Road.

A Show for the Rich; A Show for the Poor; A Show for the Old; A Show for the Young! A Show for EVERYBODY.

☞ *NOTE OUR EXCELLENT PROGRAMME FOR TO-NIGHT AND SEE THAT WE CARRY IT OUT TO THE LETTER.* ☜

PROGRAMME:

OVERTURE—"San Souci."—By our Parlor Orchestra.

Next we have a —REAL LIVE DUDE.— Dudey Delineations. "Chawles Augustus," the Dude, by - - **John Ringling.**

Now a few minutes with AMERICA'S CORNET VIRTUOSO, rendering Levy's and Arbuckle's difficult solos, - - **Alf. Ringling.**

Then comes the MAN SERPENT, the boneless wonder, the wonder of the 19th century, the limberest man known, **Mr. Fred C. Hall.**

After which we will have some very refined and pleasing clog exercises, showing how the boys and girls dance in Lancastershire, by the champion clog dancer of the world, - - - - **Abe Sands.**

Trombone Solo selected, discoursing difficult selections on his new "gold and silver" Trombone, - - - **Chas. Ringling.**

What did John, Charles, and Alf Ringling do at the hall show?

prove that they were honest. They needed to convince their audience that the Ringlings performed a family show, and that they would give a good performance that was worth the price of the ticket.

The next winter, 1883–1884, the Ringlings simply called their show, "Ringling Brothers Grand Carnival of Fun." By that time they had convinced Otto to join them as their advance agent. Now the 5 brothers who would become the famous 5 partners of the Ringling Brothers Circus—Al, Alf T., Charles, John, and Otto—worked together for the first time.

What kind of acts did the Ringlings perform?

That winter they put on 185 shows throughout the Midwest, traveling as far as Nebraska.

At the end of the season, when they totaled their income and finished paying their bills, they agreed they had enough money to realize their dreams. They could now start their own tent circus! They quickly put an advertisement in a New York magazine: "Wanted. Gymnasts, Acrobats, Leapers, **Contortionists** (kuhn **tor** shun ists), Tumblers and people in all branches of the circus business. Address Al Ringling, Baraboo, Wisconsin."

How exciting it must have been for the 5 Ringling brothers in the spring of 1884, when their long-sought dream was about to become a reality at last.

contortionist: person who can twist their body into unusual positions

3

The First Ringling Big Top

The Ringlings soon got busy bringing their circus to life. They bought lumber and made seats and supports. They purchased 3 **secondhand** farm wagons, one to be used by their advance agent and 2 to travel with the circus. For the advance agent's wagon, they painted the name of their circus

No circus is complete without an elephant!

secondhand: owned by another person first, used

on the side and made a canvas cover. They paid a farmer a few dollars and went into his forest to cut tent poles. They cut wooden stakes, which were about 4 feet long, in a nearby oak grove. The brothers removed the bark from the tent poles and stakes using a special knife and left the stakes and poles outside to dry. When the circus tents were put up, ropes holding up the tents were tied to the stakes. The stakes were pounded into the ground. The result was the first Ringling "big top" circus tent.

"Yankee" Robinson helped the Ringling brothers start their first circus.

The summer before, in 1883, Al Ringling had worked for the "Yankee" Robinson circus. Al convinced Robinson, who was then 66 years old, to help the Ringlings start their circus. The boys hoped that the well-known Yankee Robinson name would draw attention to their new show.

During the first warm days in May, everyone in the Baraboo area

For 25 cents, how many acts could you see at "The Old Yankee Robinson and Ringling Brothers Double Show"?

looked forward to the opening of the new Ringling Circus. The Ringlings' main tent, the big top, was 45 feet wide by 90 feet long. This is about as large as a high school basketball court. It could seat 600 **spectators**.

As the first show's eager audience crowded under the canvas, one seating section collapsed! Several people fell to the ground. Yankee Robinson rushed to the site of the near **calamity** (kah **lam** it tee), cracking jokes and helping people up. Workers put the seats back in order. No one was seriously hurt.

After the audience was back in their seats, Robinson gave a speech. He said the Ringling

spectator: person who watches an event but does not take part in it   **calamity:** an acciddent or disaster

23

A group of circus performers in 1890, in costume and ready to perform

brothers were "destined to become the greatest circus in the world." With that, the Ringling Brothers Circus was **launched**.

The show included jugglers, tightrope walkers, and comedy acts mixed with musical selections played by a small circus band. The Ringling boys also performed in the show. They played various instruments in the band, danced, and led several of the acrobatic stunts and tricks.

launched: started or introduced

A reporter from a local newspaper wrote about this first show: "The afternoon's business was heavy . . . In the evening the tent was crowded so that it made it **inconvenient** for them to perform." The Ringling brothers were happy that so many hometown people bought tickets to see their circus. They were pleased with their opening show in Baraboo.

That spring, the brothers hired area farm boys with their wagons and teams of horses to join the circus and travel with them. When the first show was over, the Ringlings took down the big tent, folded the canvas, pulled the stakes, took the seats apart, and loaded everything on wagons. The long tent poles stuck out far behind one wagon. The procession of 12 horse-drawn wagons trailed out of Baraboo that cool spring night, across the Baraboo Bluffs to Sauk City, their next stop.

Each day the Ringling circus performed in a new town. The little time they had for sleeping was spent in local hotels or dozing off in the wagons as they made their way along the dusty or often muddy roads. In those days there were no

inconvenient: difficult or annoying

The Ringlings traveled through beautiful, rolling countryside as they traveled from town to town.

paved roads. There were few road signs. The circus wagons, riding through the night, often got lost. Sometimes an **outrider** rode in advance, marking the road. At a fork in the road, he might borrow a rail from a nearby fence and place it across the road that wasn't to be taken. If no fence was nearby, the outrider might use pieces of paper weighted down by rocks or a handful of flour to mark the way.

On rainy nights, the workmen packed up wet tents and lifted the heavy, dripping canvas onto wagons as a team of cold, wet horses stood by. They drove all night through the

outrider: a circus employee on horseback who rode ahead of the circus

rain and gloom, with no sounds but horses plodding along and the creak of wagon wheels turning through the mud.

On such cold, wet nights, many tired farm boys quit the circus life and turned their teams and wagons toward home. They remembered the warm, dry beds that they had left a few weeks earlier. The Ringlings constantly needed to hire new help to replace those boys whose excitement for the circus had turned to misery after one too many cold, rainy nights in the wilds of Wisconsin, Iowa, or Minnesota.

Yankee Robinson appeared in every show. But he was old and sick and sometimes hardly able to walk out to the center ring. Yankee Robinson died September 4, 1884, when the circus was in Jefferson, Iowa. The boys missed their friend and helper. Many people came to the Ringlings' circus to see Yankee Robinson. Not many people had heard of the Ringling brothers yet.

Robinson's death was a turning point for the Ringling brothers. If their circus was to succeed, they would have to

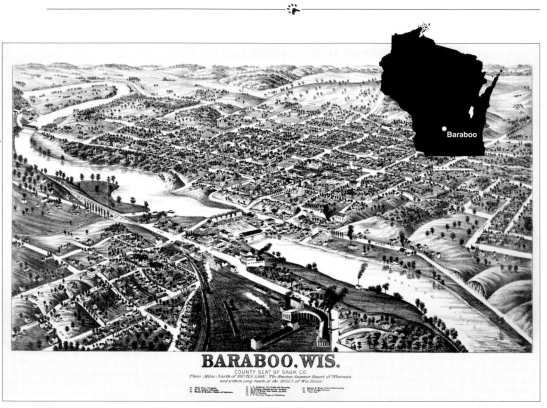

BARABOO, WIS.
COUNTY SEAT OF SAUK CO.
Three Miles North of DEVILS LAKE. The Famous Summer Resort of Wisconsin.
and within easy reach of the DELLS of Wis. River.

A birds-eye view of Baraboo, where the Ringlings made their winter home

do it on their own. They would have to make sure the tents went up on time and that the performances were perfect. The brothers themselves would have to take care of the hundreds of details needed to make a circus work.

On they drove into September, performing in Iowa and Illinois and finally Wisconsin. When the last show was over

28

on September 27, 1884, the circus returned to Baraboo for the long winter.

The Ringling Brothers Circus had played 114 towns in 4 states and had been on the road for 19 weeks. Upon arriving in Baraboo, the boys stored their equipment and began planning the 1885 season. They put the wild animals in cages in a heated building. A special barn housed their horses. They stored the tents, tent poles, ropes, and stakes in a big shed. Likewise, they stored the tent seats in a building so they would be protected from the winter snows.

The Ringling brothers had learned many things this first year on the road with their circus. First, they learned that they could put on a circus show 6 days a week, traveling from town to town. Next, they learned how to hire and manage people to help them run their show. Finally, the 5 brothers also learned how to get along with each other during good *and* bad times. All the while they were becoming better circus performers.

The Ringlings put up many **handbills** like this one to let people know the circus was coming to town.

Running a circus wasn't always easy. The long days were sometimes filled with disappointment, which came often as rainstorms drove away crowds and muddy roads made travel nearly impossible. They learned how important it was to keep going, especially when times grew tough.

But over time things got easier, too. Their circus got bigger and better, with many improvements along the way. The Ringling brothers earned all the money they needed for improvements from ticket sales. No rich person **invested** in

handbill: a small, printed advertising flyer   **invested:** gave or lent money to something, such as a company, in the belief that you would get more money back in the future

or gave them money for their circus, as was the case with some new businesses. That meant the brothers could put the money they had earned back into the circus.

From 1884 to 1889, the Ringlings developed outstanding performances for the big top. They hired clowns, acrobats, dancers, and animal trainers. They also created a traveling zoo called a **menagerie** (muh **naj** ur ee). No more kittens and English sparrows. Many country people had never seen the wild animals the Ringlings displayed. By 1889, the Ringlings had 2 elephants, 2 camels, 3 lions, a hyena, an elk, deer, a South American anteater, kangaroo, **zebu** (**zee** boo), an **emu**, birds, monkeys, and 80 horses and ponies. They had purchased all of these animals using their circus **profits**.

On September 6, 1886, a month before his 18th birthday, Henry joined his older brothers. Now, 6 of the 7 Ringling brothers would be working together.

menagerie: a collection of wild or exotic animals put on display for an audience   **zebu:** a type of ox from India with a large hump over the shoulders   **emu:** a large bird from Australia that runs, but does not fly
profit: money left over after expenses are subtracted from money made

4

A Circus on the Rails

Unlike the riverboat circus that first delighted them, the early Ringling circus was an **overland** circus. It traveled along roads and trails in farm wagons. The Ringlings continued their overland circus until the summer of 1890. That's when they reached a major decision. They decided to travel by railroad rather than with farm wagons. Once again, they were about to make another of Al's dreams come true.

The Ringling train cars were loaded with circus wagons that would travel from the train yard to the showgrounds. Can you make out the words on the side of each car?

overland: over, by, or through land, rather than by train or by boat

The Ringlings boasted about their "Enormous Railroad Shows."

The Ringlings called their 1890 show "Ringling Brothers' United Monster Railroad Shows, Menagerie and Museum." Rather than traveling from town to town by wagon, now they traveled in 18 railcars pulled by steam locomotives. In 1890, their menagerie featured 3 elephants, 3 camels, a **water buffalo**, a zebra, a zebu, a hippopotamus, several monkeys, deer, 2 wolves, a couple of boa constrictors, and additional animals making up 15 cages. The show also included 107 horses and ponies. That's a lot of animals to haul by rail!

About this time, they began calling their small **portable** city of people and animals Ringlingville.

water buffalo: a black buffalo found in Asia with long curved horns   **portable:** able to be moved

33

Al Ringling's wife, Lou, was an early snake charmer with the Ringling Brothers circus.

Ringlingville was really a city under canvas. It had its own barber shop, general store, dining hall, post office, and blacksmith shop—everything found in a regular city. Except this city moved 6 days a week!

Traveling by train, the Ringling Brothers Circus could now reach audiences almost anywhere in the country. In 1890, besides traveling throughout the upper Midwest, the brothers put on shows in Indiana, Ohio, Pennsylvania, Maryland, Virginia, and West Virginia. The Ringling brothers had never before traveled in these states. They wondered if people would come to their circus. But come they did. People came by the thousands! While they were in

Ringlingville's own traveling barbershop

Punxsutawney (punk suh **taw** nee), Pennsylvania, the circus
had to close the ticket wagon half an hour before the show
started because there were no more seats. When the
Ringling brothers returned their circus to Baraboo in the fall
of 1890 for the winter, they were pleased. Their circus had
been in more states than ever before, and more people had
attended than in any previous year.

Each year the Ringling Brothers Circus grew larger. By 1915, the circus traveled on 85 railcars that moved in 4 sections, each section pulled by a steam locomotive. From a penny circus in a neighbor's barn to a world famous, not-to-be-missed event, the Ringling Brothers Circus had come a long way. Now it could truly be called a great success!

Mail call! Ringlingville's post office was in a circus wagon.

5

The Circus Comes to Town

It was an exciting time when the circus came to town. Families turned out by the hundreds to see the Ringlings unload their railcars and move the equipment to the show grounds. Watching the Ringling crew put up the tents was even more exciting. Here's how it all happened.

Ringlingville, a city of tents, waits for the circus crowds to arrive.

Weeks before the circus arrived in a town, the advance man visited the town to ask local businesses to provide feed, such as hay and grain, for the circus animals. He also ordered groceries for the circus cook tent. Here is what the advance man ordered for the circus kitchen before the circus came to Duluth, Minnesota, in 1908:

* 90 gallons of fresh milk
* 20 gallons of evaporated milk
* 1,000 pounds of bread
* 300 pounds of steak, ham, young lamb chops, and veal
* 90 pounds of butter
* 45 bushels of potatoes
* 18 bushels of spinach and young beets
* 250 dozen eggs
* 35 pounds of American cheese
* 100 pounds of rice pudding
* 300 pies of 4 varieties

The day the circus came to town the circus train's first section, called the "Flying Squadron," arrived at the rail yard in the still dark hour before sunup. It carried the kitchen and dining tents, chef, cooks, equipment, and helpers. The train engineer carefully eased the 20-some circus cars onto a sidetrack for unloading. Sometimes several hundred local people gathered to watch.

A circus worker known as the "24-hour man" met the train. He showed the early arrivals to the show grounds, which was sometimes a half-mile or farther away. The show

Thousands of people came to see the circus perform in the big top.

grounds were usually empty town lots or farmers' fields on the edge of town. The 24-hour man arrived the day before to make sure everything was in order at the rail yard and the show site. He visited the local shops that had agreed to provide feed and other supplies to remind them that the circus was coming. The businesses would need to deliver everything the 24-hour man ordered. The 24-hour man also checked the streets the circus wagons would travel on to make sure the wagons would have no difficulty getting through to the show grounds. These wagons would haul tents, animals, and equipment from the rail yard.

Circus goers could buy pink lemonade, popcorn, peanuts, and Cracker Jacks at the Parson Brothers candy stand.

In 1915, the Ringling Brothers Circus included 17 tents. When they were put up they covered 14 acres of land. That's as much land as 12 football fields! The tents were used for many different things. The biggest and most important tent was the big top, where the main performance took place. There was 1 tent for the animal menagerie, and 1 for the sideshow. There were 3 horse tents and 1 pony tent. There were 3 dining tents and 1 cook tent. There were also 2 dressing tents, a ballet tent, and a wardrobe tent. More tents were needed for candy and souvenier stands.

WHI IMAGE ID 33797

By 1910, the Ringling Brothers circus had 500 Percheron horses like this one, which is just a colt.

Back at the rail yard, workmen began unloading the horses, which wore their harnesses on the train. Other men immediately began unloading circus wagons from the railcars. **Percheron (per** chuh ron) horses—in teams of 4, 6,

Percheron horse: a breed of powerful, rugged work horse from France

and 8—were quickly hitched to the wagons and began pulling them to the show grounds.

The workers finished unloading the first section of the train just as the second section arrived. The train engineer switched this train into position and workers continued unloading. Horses, wagons, and workers were everywhere. Lions roared; elephants trumpeted. **Exotic** sounds filled the early morning air. The smells of dust, horse sweat, and **manure** hung in the air as the teams of horses leaned into

PHOTO BY H.W. PELTON

How many horses does it take to pull a wagon full of tents and poles?

exotic: strange and fascinating, often from a faraway place   **manure:** the waste that animals leave behind

An elephant stepping off a rail car

their harnesses and pulled the heavy wagons toward the circus grounds. Townspeople who watched were amazed at what they saw.

The boss "canvasman" — the man in charge of **erecting** tents—arrived at the show grounds ahead of the others and began marking the location for each of the 17 tents. He carried with him a sketch of which tent should go where. He instructed the layout gang to set hundreds of small, 2- to 3-foot-long iron pins which showed where each tent should go.

Workers first put up the cook and dining tents. Then they started fires in the coal-burning kitchen stoves. Soon bacon and eggs were frying. The smell sharpened the appetites of workers putting up other tents. Other workers drew water from the water wagon and poured it into giant black kettles that sat above crackling wood fires outside the

erecting: putting up a structure or building

43

cook tent. In minutes coffee was boiling. The circus employees drank 185 quarts of coffee and 65 gallons of tea each day. Nine cooks worked under the direction of the head chef and prepared all the food. In less than an hour, waiters dressed in white would be ready to serve breakfast to the hungry crew.

Wagons carrying tent poles and horse tents arrived. Men placed the huge center poles where they would be raised, while others erected the horse tents. As soon as the

Waiters in the performer's dining tent

Workers took turns driving the massive stakes into the ground.

horses were rested and cooled from their early morning work, they were fed and given water.

Working in crews of 6, stake drivers took their positions around 4-foot-long, 2- to 3-inch-thick wooden stakes. These stakes would hold the great tents in place. One by one, each muscular man struck a stake with a huge hammer. The air was filled with the "bang, bang, bang" sound of hammering. In just 45 minutes, some 30 stake drivers pounded in as many as 1,000 stakes.

The big top was the largest of all the tents. It was 440 feet long (longer than a football field) and about 190 feet wide. It seated more than 12,000 people. It took 20 to 30 men, with the help of many horses and elephants, to raise its

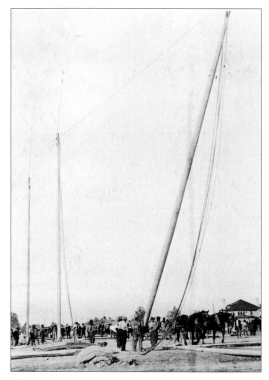

The tall center poles went up before the big top tent could be lifted into place.

center poles. While the center poles were going up, other workers spread the canvas on the ground and laced together the center pieces. Then they raised the side poles, and shoved them into special pockets in the canvas. They tied ropes to each of these and attached the ropes to stakes in the ground.

Next, several men gathered at the middle of the tent and with ropes and **pulleys** began pulling the tent up the center poles. After they raised the tent a few feet, they hitched a team of horses or sometimes an elephant to the ropes. The animals quickly pulled the tent to its full height. Soon all the other tents were up. In just a few hours, the flat, empty land of the show grounds had been

pulley: wheel with a groove on the outside in which a chain or rope can run, used to lift heavy objects

It took a lot of workers to spread the canvas before the tent was lifted from the ground.

What performers do you see atop this colorful circus wagon?

transformed into a small city of tents. Ringlingville was ready to go!

By this time breakfast was ready. The crews filed into the dining tents. They had already worked several hours. When they finished eating, the performers and

47

The entire town turned out to see the circus parade.

workmen began to prepare for the circus parade scheduled for 11 a.m. The parade would wind its way along the town streets to attract audiences for the day's 2 big top shows, at 2 and 8 p.m. Spectators lined the streets to stare up at the colorful circus wagons. Some of the wagons carried wild animals such as lions and tigers. Others carried circus performers in bright, exotic costumes. The townspeople also heard and saw a circus band playing spirited tunes. Elephants paraded by as well as horses with shiny leather harnesses. Clowns were everywhere, delighting children with their **antics**.

antic: playful or funny action

Sideshow performers included the fat man, tattooed man, bagpiper, and a snake charmer.

Before the big top show, those who bought tickets
took in an hour-long band concert in the big top or toured
the circus menagerie and sideshow tents, all part of the
50-cent (25 cents for children) admission price.

In the sideshow tent, you might see the "thinnest
person alive" or a snake charmer performing. On the circus
grounds you could buy peanuts, popcorn, and pink lemonade

from the concession stand. And if you had any extra money you could buy a circus souvenir, such as a toy elephant or a brightly decorated cane.

The first big top show started at 2 p.m. sharp. The ringmaster blew his whistle, and in a loud voice said, "Ladies and gentlemen, children of all ages." It was the traditional way of welcoming people to the circus. The ringmaster then

The main entrance to the big top tent

Jules Turnour, one of the Ringling clowns, in street clothes
and in clown makeup

introduced the first event—a colorful parade of animals and
performers, a hint of what was to come. This first event was
called a **spectacle** (**spek** tuh kul).

For the next 2 hours, **awestruck** visitors saw high-
wire **aerialists** (**air** ee uh lists) swinging high up in the
tent. In 3 different rings they watched jugglers, bareback
riders, and elephants perform. They laughed at the tricks of

spectacle: a remarkable or dramatic sight   **awestruck:** filled with wonder
aerialist: person who performs in the air or above the ground

51

All of these women, including the girl in the middle of the photo, were circus performers. Would you like to have worked for the circus?

dozens of clowns. A live orchestra played during the entire performance.

When the afternoon show was over, workers and performers had a few short hours to rest. Then they ate their dinner before the crowds arrived for the evening show. The evening show began promptly at 8 p.m.

Like the shows themselves, everything was tightly organized so that the circus could move quickly to the next town. Even before the evening program began, workers began taking down the cook tents and horse tents and loading them on wagons for the trip back to the rail yard. The first section of the circus train then started its journey to the next town. It would arrive well ahead of the rest of the circus.

Workers lowered the sideshow tent about 8 p.m. They closed the menagerie and moved the animals and the sideshow tent to the train at 9 p.m. Soon the second section of the train was on its way to the next town. By the end of the evening performance, all that remained standing were the big top and dressing room tents.

When the evening show was over, the boss canvasman blew his whistle. Workers quickly began taking down the big top. They lowered the lights, which hung from the ceiling, and loosened the ropes that held the canvas to the center pole. The big tent slowly eased to the ground.

The men then unlaced the tent pieces, rolled the huge sections of canvas into bundles, and loaded them into wagons. They lowered the center poles and yanked the hundreds of stakes out of the ground. Soon the last stake was loaded, and the remaining wagons lumbered off to the rail yard to catch the last section of the train. The other train sections had already left about a half hour apart.

The next day, and the day after that, and every day except Sunday, from April to November, these traveling circus workers would repeat this same routine. They knew how to do all the tasks as **efficiently** (eh **fish** unt lee) as possible. How were the Ringling brothers able to make all of this work so well? Moving a circus required vast knowledge of everything from railroad schedules to handling hundreds of animals. The Ringling brothers divided the many jobs, so that each one took responsibility for one big job.

efficiently: not wasting time or energy

6
Meet the Ringling Brothers

Each Ringling brother had a special job. Each did what he liked to do, and together they made a great team. Five of

The five Ringling brothers who owned the circus were often pictured together: Alf T., Al, John, Otto, and Charles.

the brothers—Al, Otto, Alf T., Charles, and John—were business partners. But they never had a written agreement. They simply agreed to divide the circus expenses and profits 5 ways. Two other brothers, Gus and Henry, worked as employees of the circus. But as we will see, they also had important jobs. Different from some families, the 7 Ringling brothers got along well with each other. They knew that if their circus was to succeed, they must not squabble. The 5 brothers who were partners in the Ringling Brothers Circus even looked alike. Each wore a bushy mustache.

Albert "Al" Ringling (1852–1916), Partner

Al, the oldest of the Ringling brothers, was in charge of hiring and supervising the circus performers. As ringmaster for many years, he was in front of all the circus audiences,

announcing the acts and making sure everything ran according to schedule. He was in charge of the twice-a-day performances held in the big top. Al was a perfectionist, which meant he wanted everything to go just the way he wanted, perfectly!

Al Ringlng

Al was very strict, but he also had a soft side, and he enjoyed helping people. One time he noticed a woman who was crying. She had a little girl with her, and they were hurrying away from the show grounds. Al caught up to her and asked her what was wrong. She said that she had lost her purse, which contained 3 dollars and her railroad tickets home. Al motioned for one of his men and instructed him to take the woman and her daughter to the show and sit with them in the best seats. After the performance the man was to escort them to the best hotel for supper, buy the woman a new purse, **reimburse** her lost money, and even buy train tickets for their trip back home.

Al loved Baraboo, Wisconsin, where he made his home. While several of his other brothers had homes elsewhere, Al always lived in Baraboo when he was not on the road. His big house still stands just off Baraboo's downtown square. Al **financed** the building of the magnificent Al Ringling Theater in Baraboo. You can still see this theater today and attend shows there.

No matter where the circus happened to be, when Al had some free time, he went fishing. When he died in 1916, part of the Ringling Brothers Circus died with him. He was the one who wanted to start a circus way back when he and

reimburse: to pay someone back the money he or she spent or lost
financed: provided money for something

The Al Ringling Theater today

his brothers were kids. Without him, there might have been no Ringling Brothers Circus.

William "Otto" Ringling (1858–1911), Partner

Always fond of numbers, Otto was treasurer for the circus. This meant he managed all the money that came in and all the money that was spent. Some would say he was stingy. Others called his behavior **frugal** (**fru** gul). Otto became a genius at working with money. This allowed the

frugal: careful and thoughtful about how one spends money

58

Ringling Brothers Circus to become the largest in the world. Otto was quiet and loved good books, so he built a large personal library. He never married, and he never owned a

home. When he wasn't on the road with the circus, he lived with his brother Alf T., where he kept his books. His brothers sometimes called Otto the "King" because he and he alone controlled the Ringling brothers' money. But he was fair and honest. He never

Otto Ringlng   cheated his brothers or anyone else.

Alfred Theodore "Alf T." Ringling (1863–1919)

Alf T. was in charge of working with newspapers to advertise and promote the circus. He knew hundreds of newspaper editors throughout the United States and Canada. He also supervised the writers who worked for the circus just writing news articles about it. They sent their stories to newspapers before

Alf T. Ringlng   the circus arrived in a town. When people in

59

the town read the circus stories, they grew more excited about attending the circus. In other words, the stories helped sell more tickets.

Alf T. took part in all major decision-making but he left day-to-day circus operations to Al, Charles, and Otto. Alf T. played the cornet and loved to fish. During the circus's wagon-show days he played in the circus band. For several years he wrote the annual circus route books. The route books were a diary or journal that told about each town where the circus played, anything special that happened, and how many people came to each show. He also wrote a book, *Life Story of the Ringling Brothers*, in 1900. This was one of the first histories of the Ringling Brothers Circus.

Carl "Charles" Ringling (1864–1926), Partner

Charles was in charge of more than 70 men who put up billboards, posters, and signs that advertised the circus. They traveled ahead of the circus to put up these colorful posters. Posters came both small and large. Sometimes

Charles Ringlng

they were small enough to fit in store windows and sometimes they were 20 or more feet long and 10 feet high. Posters showed circus animals, performers, and clowns in vivid colors. They announced times and places where the circus would appear.

Charles also worked behind the scenes to keep the circus operating smoothly and efficiently. He was a favorite

A bill poster at work

among all the circus employees, workers as well as performers. He spent a great deal of time walking from tent to tent, visiting and chatting with everyone connected to the circus. The staff affectionately referred to him as Mr. Charlie.

These posters advertised the circus's June 13, 1899, arrival in Manchester, New Hampshire.

If there was a problem, no matter how large or small, circus workers knew they could go to Charles for help.

Charles was the most musically talented of the brothers. Once a season, up to the year before he died, he played a **baritone** solo with the circus band. He also collected rare and expensive violins. In his spare time, Charles went fishing.

baritone: a horn whose musical range and size is between the trumpet and the tuba

John Ringling (1866–1936), Partner

John Ringlng

John planned where the circus would perform each year. The Ringling Brothers Circus owned its own railcars, but not the engines that pulled them. The circus had to pay to travel on a railroad's tracks. John was in charge of working with small and large railroads across the country. He became an expert on where railroads ran and who ran them.

John always wore the finest clothes available. Some called him a show-off. John did not like Baraboo. He felt that the town was too small for him. While his brothers were still living in Baraboo, he lived in a hotel in Chicago. He later lived in New York City.

During the winter John traveled all over Europe on the lookout for outstanding circus acts that he could recommend to his brother Al. John also became an art collector and bought many fine paintings. Today these are in an art museum in Sarasota, Florida, in John's former mansion. John also bought more than 100,000 acres of ranch land in Montana and Oklahoma and founded the towns of Ringling, Montana, and Ringling, Oklahoma. He wanted people to remember the Ringling name, no matter where they lived.

Augustus "A. G." or "Gus" Ringling (1854–1907)

Gus worked for his 5 brothers who ran the Ringling Brothers Circus. He was not a partner. He joined the older brothers in 1890 when the circus became a railroad circus. Although he wasn't "in charge," he had a very important job.

He supervised Advertising Railcar No. 1. His job included managing 27 men who were responsible for pasting circus advertising on the barns and sheds across the country. Gus read many books, and some said he was the most gentle of the brothers.

Gus Ringlng

The advertising cars rode a few weeks ahead to put up posters on fences and barns.

Henry Ringling (1868–1918)

Henry Ringlng

Henry was the youngest of the brothers. He was also the largest. He was 6-foot 3-inches tall and weighed more than 300 pounds. He joined the show in 1886 and later became superintendent of the main entrance to the big top. This meant he supervised the ticket takers and made sure those without tickets did not enter. When Otto died in 1911, he left his share of the circus to Henry. Henry then became a partner.

Because each Ringling brother had his own job in the circus and did it well, the circus thrived. It was also important that the brothers respected each other's decisions. This wasn't always easy. Just like any other family, they

Imagine how much teamwork it took to get the circus ready each day!

sometimes disagreed. This often happened at the end of the year when they were deciding where the circus would perform and which acts they would feature in the coming year. Each brother shared his opinion. When a decision was finally made, there were no more arguments.

Through their entire lives, the Ringling brothers kept working on their skills and talents. They knew that to compete with other circuses, they would have to constantly improve. And they did. They never stopped learning how to do their jobs better. The brothers knew that one brother's job was not more important than the others. They considered all their jobs of equal importance to the success of the circus.

For years the brothers knew that if their circus was to continue succeeding, each brother needed to work hard. Probably because they were so poor as children and had so little money when their circus first opened, the brothers never considered retiring. So they kept working hard, even when they got older and had lots of money.

Family also was very important to the Ringling brothers. At the end of each show season, all of the Ringlings and their families gathered in Baraboo for a festive Christmas party. During the summer, when the circus was on the road, the brothers' wives and children often traveled with the circus. What fun that must have been! The brothers also helped circus workers when there was an illness or injury by stepping in to pay their bills.

7

The Ringling Menagerie

The Ringling brothers loved animals. They also knew that people came to the circus to see animals they had never seen before. At the Ringling circus, people saw wild animals from all around the United States and from other parts of the

What animals can you identify in the circus menagerie?

Feeding time for the giraffes!

world. By 1915, the Ringling brothers' menagerie included elephants, giraffes, hippos, tigers, lions, **yaks**, zebus, zebras, **ibexes**, water buffaloes, deer, boa constrictors, wolves, camels, **gnus** (nooz) , antelopes, kangaroos, and a rhinoceros. The Ringling brothers bought many of these animals from an animal dealer in Germany. The animal dealer paid trappers to capture wild animals, especially in Africa.

People who came to the circus also liked to watch trained horses and dogs, as well as other animals, perform in the big top show ring. Visitors to the circus enjoyed seeing elephants help put up the circus tent poles and push wagons that got stuck in the mud. They loved seeing elephants walking in the circus parade and performing in the big top tent. A newspaper reporter described the elephants' role in

yak: a type of ox from central Asia with long, dark shaggy hair   **ibex:** a type of wild mountain goat from Asia and North Africa with large, ridged horns   **gnu:** an antelope from Africa with a head like an ox, a short mane, a long tail, and horns

If you worked for the circus, would you like to train zebras too?

the circus parade: "Each beast grasped the tail of the animal in front of him with his trunk and held on like grim death. Well ahead of the elephants a man on horseback rode by yelling, 'Friends, **secure** your horses tightly! The elephants are about to pass by.'"

In those days, everyone traveled either on horseback or in a horse-drawn vehicle. Horses became frightened at the smell of an elephant. Sometimes the horses ran away, causing injury and damage to buggies and wagons. The phrase "hold your horses" comes from these times.

secure: to keep safe or well protected, to hold

71

In 1888, the Ringling brothers bought their first elephants and named them Babylon (**Bab** ih lon) and Fannie. This was 4 years after they started their circus. Some people said a circus wasn't a real circus until it had at least

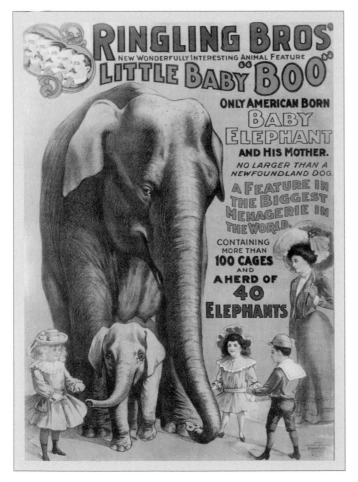

An ad for the Ringling's new baby elephant

1 elephant. When the Ringlings got their first elephants, they were still an overland circus. This meant they walked from town to town, carrying their equipment on horse-drawn wagons. It also meant that the elephants walked from town to town. Imagine the sight of a parade of wagons, complete with elephants, on a normally deserted country road!

In 1892, 2 years after the Ringlings became a railroad circus, the brothers owned 6 elephants. By 1908 they had 40 of these huge beasts in their elephant herd. On November 19, 1900, an amazing event occurred at the winter headquarters in Baraboo. A baby elephant was born, the first one in Baraboo. A magazine reporter

Trimming an elephant's toenails was no small task.

wrote: "The Ringling Bros. are without question the proudest and happiest showmen in America today. The baby elephant is of course the cause of this joy. And such a dear little baby he is. A perfect miniature elephant, 34 inches long weighing 300 pounds, carrying a trunk one foot in length . . . Little Nick was born about 4:30 Monday morning, only a few hours after the show arrived in winter quarters."

Another famous Ringling Brothers Circus animal was a hippopotamus named Pete. It was the first hippo the Ringlings owned. He weighed 4,800 pounds. That's as heavy as 2 cars put together! In advertisements, they described their big hippo as "the indescribable, tremendous monster of **brute** creation, the largest hippopatamus in **captivity**" This statement was probably not true, because the Ringlings had no way of knowing if their hippo was the largest in captivity.

The Ringling brothers' first rhinoceros was named Mary. She weighed about 4,000

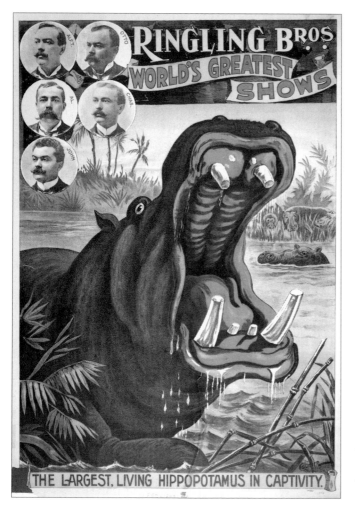

Meet the Ringling hippo, Pete!

brute: rough and violent   **captivity:** the state of being held or kept, like animals in a zoo

The Ringling rhinoceros, Mary, was a popular attraction.

pounds and had to be fed a special diet. The animal keepers had very careful instructions on how to care for her: "After giving her water in the morning, prepare a mash. Make the mash by cutting 3 loaves of bread into coarse cubes, add ½ dozen carrots, ½ dozen potatoes, ½ head of cabbage, one pint of **bran**, and ½ handful of salt. In the afternoon, after watering her again, give her a bundle of hay, about 16 pounds. Expect that she will drink about 24 quarts of water at a time. This is about 1½ pails of water."

bran: the outer covering of wheat that is left over when flour is made

Mike Rooney, a talented bareback performer

Horses were the most common animals the Ringling Brothers Circus owned. At one time, 500 horses traveled with the circus. Most of them were work horses, called "baggage **stock**". They pulled the heavy circus wagons from the train yard to the show grounds. They also pulled wagons in the circus parade and helped the workers put up the circus tents. A much smaller number were show horses, called "ring stock". These horses had specially trained riders who performed stunts while the horses raced around the

stock: cattle, sheep, pigs, and other animals typically used on a ranch or farm

show ring. Sometimes they performed without riders by doing dances, standing on their back legs, or doing other tricks to entertain the audience.

Show dogs, usually little ones, were also part of the Ringling Brothers Circus. At one time, Al Ringling trained show dogs and put on an act with them. Trained dogs did somersaults, raced around the show ring, jumped through hoops, stood on pails, and performed many other tricks that circus audiences enjoyed.

During the early days of the circus, Al Ringling trained dogs to jump through hoops and climb ladders.

A sixteen-camel hitch was quite a sight to see.

The Ringling brothers believed that a circus was not complete without animals—even though they required lots of special care and training. The brothers were always proud of how well their employees treated the animals. They even hired a veterinarian to travel with the circus and make sure that all the animals stayed healthy.

During the winter months, all the Ringling animals lived in Baraboo, at the Ringling Brothers' Winter Quarters. It must have been quite an effort to keep the animals well-fed, comfortable, and warm all winter long.

8

Winter Quarters

Each fall when the Ringling Brothers Circus finished
the season, the circus trains returned to the small town of
Baraboo, Wisconsin. This was usually in October or
November, when it got too cold to hold a circus outdoors in
most parts of the country. The Ringlings first **wintered** their

Winter quarters in Baraboo, 1905

wintered: kept, fed, or managed during the winter

circus in Baraboo in 1884–1885. Their last winter in Baraboo was 1917–1918. Altogether, the Ringling Brothers Circus spent 33 winters in Baraboo.

The Ringling winter quarter buildings lined up along the banks of the Baraboo River on the south side of Baraboo. When the Ringling circus trains arrived in Baraboo in the fall, workmen quickly unloaded the railcars containing animals and made them comfortable in their winter quarters.

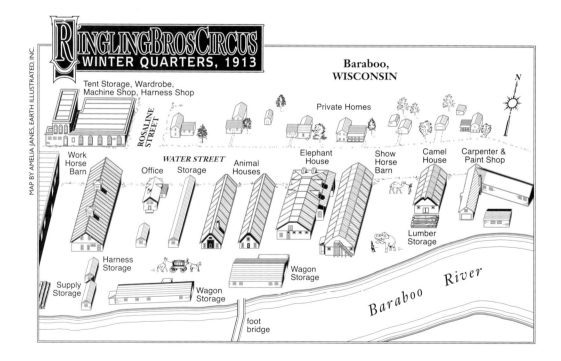

Winter quarters included special heated buildings for the elephants, giraffes, lions, tigers, pythons, and panthers. Special unheated barns housed the horses, camels, zebras and other hay-eating animals.

The tents, tent poles, bleachers, and ropes were all stored away for the winter. Huge sheds housed the circus wagons, and a special railroad shop, with rails running through it, sheltered the 85 railcars of the circus train. It usually took from 2 to 3 weeks for the Ringling brothers and the circus workers to store everything in the various buildings.

As many as 1,200 people worked for the Ringling Brothers Circus during the show season. This number included the show people and those who worked behind the scenes. Behind-the-scenes workers put up and took down tents, cared for the horses, and cooked and served meals for the workers. Others worked as barbers and blacksmiths. Naturally, the winter crew was much smaller. For one thing, the circus didn't need the performers during the winter.

Most of the people who stayed with the circus were behind-the-scenes workers. The chart below shows the number of people who worked as winter employees in 1913–1914.

These 117 employees worked during the long, cold winter months to repair equipment and make the circus ready for the next season. Most of the performers worked at other jobs during the winter. They did not live in Baraboo, but returned to the Ringling Brothers Circus in the spring, around April. Some worked at indoor shows in other parts of the country. Some took the winter off for vacation. Many of the workmen also took other jobs during the winter. Some of them worked in northern

Winter Employees	
Caring for the work horses	23
Caring for the show horses	7
Caring for menagerie animals	8
Elephant caretakers	10
Blacksmiths	5
Railcar repair	16
Paint shop	16
Harness shop	3
Wagon and repair shop	9
Wardrobe	5
Hotel	12
Watchmen	2
Office	1
Total	**117**

Wisconsin at lumber camps. But almost all of them returned to Baraboo in the spring, to work once again for the Ringling brothers and their circus.

Some of the workmen repaired and made new equipment during the winter months. Others worked with the show animals, especially the elephants and the horses. Pearl Souder was the Ringling elephant trainer for many years. He said that elephants, just like people, developed soft

Even the elephants needed to practice during the long winter months.

RALPH PIERCE COLLECTION

The "mechanic," a device used to train horses and riders

and flabby muscles if they did not exercise. At one end of the elephant building, a special area was set aside for the elephants to exercise. Sometimes, if the weather was mild, they exercised outside. Their exercises usually included the tricks they performed during the regular circus season—performing handstands, standing on a single foot, walking on their hind legs, and sitting down. Townspeople from Baraboo usually were not allowed to watch the elephant trainers work. The close quarters made it too dangerous for visitors.

At one end of the show horse barn was a training area for horses and riders. The show horses, just like the elephants, needed regular exercise to keep them in good physical shape. The trainers also had to make sure that the horses remembered the stunts they were taught. The trainers' winter months also were used to teach both elephants and horses new tricks that would be performed during the coming season.

At winter quarters, the Ringling brothers together decided on circus acts for the coming summer, and what performers they would hire. Alf T. and Charles Ringling were both concerned about advertising for the circus and spreading the word about new acts. They worked with the staff to develop new designs for the posters to be used the next season. Often, the posters showed off dazzling new costumes for these performances. The costumes were created by the wardrobe department. When the new act was ready, a team of writers wrote news stories for the newspapers along the route where the circus would play.

The winter days were busy days for the circus people in Baraboo. It was very different from the regular show season. For one thing, there was no moving from town to town each day. There also was no money being made during the winter months because there were no performances and no tickets were sold. The Ringlings had to earn enough money during the show season to last through the winter.

In winter quarters, artists designed posters for the coming season.

If you go to Baraboo today, you can still see many of the original buildings used by the Ringlings. These buildings are a part of Circus World Museum, which is open to the public all year-round.

For many years, Circus World has remembered the Ringling brothers with a marvelous

Winter also meant new acts and new costumes, such as this one for Joan of Arc.

PHOTO BY STEVE APPS

Loading circus rail cars for the annual circus parade at Circus World

parade in Milwaukee and Baraboo. The parade is a lot like the parades from 100 years ago with brightly painted circus wagons, horses, elephants, bands, and performing clowns.

WHI IMAGE ID 24023

Teaching zebras to pull a cart at winter quarters in 1909

Imagine what it would have been like living in Baraboo during the years that the Ringling Brothers Circus wintered there. You might see elephants walking down your street as they exercised. Teams of 4, 6, or 8 horses pulling colorful circus wagons might travel by your house. You might even catch a glimpse of a team of camels pulling a wagon, or perhaps zebras harnessed to a buggy traveling along Baraboo's streets.

During the cold, dark winter nights you might hear a lion roar, an elephant trumpet, or the snarl of a tiger or panther. Those were exciting times for the people of Baraboo. Their town was the home of the Ringling Brothers Circus, the largest and greatest circus in the world.

Afterword

In the fall of 1918, the Ringling Brothers Circus train turned east rather than north toward Wisconsin. The circus would winter in Bridgeport, Connecticut, and would not return to Baraboo again. By this time, only 3 of the original 7 Ringling brothers were still alive, Alf T., Charles, and John.

In 1907, the Ringling brothers had bought the famous Barnum & Bailey Circus. From 1907 to 1918, the Ringling brothers ran both their own circus and the Barnum & Bailey Circus, which had its own winter quarters in Bridgeport, Connecticut. During the winter of 1918–1919, both circuses stayed in Bridgeport.

In 1919, the Ringling brothers decided to put the 2 circuses together. They called it "The Greatest Show on Earth." Charles and John ran the show. Alf T., who was ill, died that fall.

⁙

By 1925 the combined circus had more than 100 railcars. It clearly was the "greatest show on earth," and the largest, too! But times were still changing. Charles Ringling died in 1926, leaving John to run the big show. In 1927, John moved the circus winter quarters from Bridgeport, Connecticut, to Sarasota, Florida. John already owned a magnificent mansion in Sarasota. He owned the circus with Mrs. Charles Ringling and Alf T. Ringling's son's wife. In 1932, these 2 owners decided that John, who was ill, should no longer run the circus. They hired Sam Gumpertz as manager. It was the first time someone without the Ringling name was in charge of the circus. Gumpertz ran the show from 1932 to 1938.

The Ringling brothers had only one sister, Ida, who was the youngest in the family. She was born in 1874. Her son, John Ringling North, became manager of the huge circus in 1938, 2 years after his uncle, John Ringling, died. A true circus man, John Ringling North stayed with the circus until 1967. Those years brought even more changes. In 1956, the circus stopped showing under the big top. They began putting on their shows in auditoriums, arenas, and coliseums. Now they could have shows all seasons of the year and weather was never a problem.

In 1967 came the biggest change of all. The Irvin Feld family bought the Ringling Bros. Barnum & Bailey Circus

In 1919, the Ringling Brothers Circus and Barnum and Bailey combined into one huge show.

from the Ringling family. For the first time since 1884, no Ringling family member owned the circus or helped to run it.

Even though a new family owned the circus, they didn't change its name. Today, it is still known as "Ringling Bros. and Barnum and Bailey: The Greatest Show on Earth." The Feld family still owns the circus, which continues to travel through towns and cities all over the United States, entertaining young and old alike.

Appendix

The Ringling Brothers

The Ringling family in 1895. Standing left to right: Al, Alf T., Gus, Charles, and Otto. Seated: John, Salome, August, Ida, and Henry.

Albert "Al" Ringling (1852–1916), Partner

Al was the oldest of the brothers. He was the program director for the circus and hired the performers. For many years he was also the ringmaster, which meant he introduced each act to the crowd. Along with 4 of his brothers, he owned the Ringling Brothers Circus.

August "A.G." or "Gus" Ringling (1854–1907)

Gus, the second oldest brother, did not begin working with the circus until 1890, many years after it was started. He worked for his 5 brothers who ran the Ringling Brothers Circus. He helped advertise the circus by supervising the men who put up circus posters before the circus came to town.

William "Otto" Ringling (1858–1911), Partner

Otto was one of the 5 brothers who owned the circus. He served as treasurer and kept detailed records of all money earned and every penny spent. He became known as a "financial genius." People said he was frugal or even stingy because he was so careful with the circus money.

Alfred Theodore "Alf T." Ringling (1863–1919), Partner

Alf T., one of the 5 owners, was in charge of talking to the press about the circus. He wrote newspaper stories that he sent to newspapers around the country. He also supervised other writers who wrote news stories about the circus.

Carl "Charles" Ringling (1864–1926), Partner

Charles was in charge of advertising for the circus. He supervised an army of men who put up the posters that let everyone know the circus was coming to town. Charles also was on the circus grounds each day to make sure that the behind-the-scenes activities of the circus operated smoothly. He was one of the 5 owners.

John Ringling (1866–1936), Partner

John decided where the circus would travel each year. He was an expert on where railroads went and who ran them. As one of the 5 owners, he helped decide where and when the circus would have shows. During the winter months, John traveled to Europe in search of new circus performers.

Henry Ringling (1868–1918)

Henry was the youngest of the 7 brothers. He joined the circus in 1886 as an employee. He became superintendent

of the main entrance to the big top, the big circus show tent.
He became an owner when his brother, Otto, died in 1911.

Ringling Time Line

1848 — August Ringling, a harness maker, arrives in Milwaukee. He was born in Germany in 1826.

1852 — August Ringling marries Salome Marie Juliar. Salome was born in France in 1833. August and Salome are the parents of the Ringling boys.

1852 — Al Ringling is born in Chicago.

1854 — Gus Ringling is born in Milwaukee.

1855–1860 — The Ringling family lives in Baraboo, Wisconsin. Otto Ringling is born in Baraboo in 1858.

1860 — The Ringling family moves to McGregor, Iowa, the birthplace of several sons: Alfred Theodore or Alf T. in 1863, Charles in 1864, John in 1866, and Henry in 1868.

1874 — Ida Ringling, the only Ringling daughter, is born in Prairie du Chien, Wisconsin.

1875 — The Ringling family moves back to Baraboo.

1882 — The Ringling boys put on their first hall show in Mazomanie, Wisconsin.

1884 – The first Ringling Brothers Circus opens in Baraboo, Wisconsin. Baraboo becomes winter quarters for their circus.

1884–1890 – The Ringling Brothers Circus travels with farm wagons. This type of circus is called an overland circus.

1888 – The Ringling Brothers Circus purchases their first elephants. Their names are Babylon and Fannie.

1890 – The Ringling Brothers Circus begins traveling on railroad cars.

1915 – The Ringling Brothers Circus has become the largest in the world. The circus includes 1,200 workers, 500 horses, 40 elephants, 85 railroad cars, 14 tents and a big top tent that can seat 12,000 people.

1918 – The Ringling Brothers Circus moves to Connecticut for the winter. It never returns to Baraboo. Their old winter quarters become Circus World Museum in 1959.

1919 – Ringling Brothers and Barnum & Bailey merge as a giant circus. They call it "The Greatest Show on Earth." It continues to this day.

Glossary

aerialist (**air** ee uh list): person who performs in the air or above the ground

antic: playful or funny action

awestruck: filled with wonder

baritone: a horn whose musical range and size is between the trumpet and the tuba

boast: to talk proudly about yourself in order to impress people

bran: the outer covering of wheat that is left over when flour is made

brute: rough and violent

calamity (kah **lam** ih tee): an accident or disaster

captivity: the state of being held or kept, like animals in a zoo

contortionist: (kuhn **tor** shun ist): person who can twist their body into unusual positions

cornet: a horn similar to a trumpet, but shorter in length

dynasty: a powerful kingdom or family that has ruled for a long time

efficiently (eh **fish** unt lee): not wasting time or energy

emu: a large bird from Australia that runs, but does not fly

entrepreneur (ahn truh preh **nur**): person who starts his or her own business from scratch

erecting: putting up a structure or building

exotic: strange and fascinating, often from a faraway place

expense: amount of money spent

financed: provided money for something

frugal (**fru** gul): careful and thoughtful about how one spends money

gnu (noo): an antelope from Africa with a head like an ox, a short mane, a long tail, and horns

handbill: a small, printed advertising flyer

house: amount of money made from ticket sales

ibex: a type of wild mountain goat from Asia and North Africa with large, ridged horns

income: amount of money made from an event or sale

imported: brought into a country from another place or region

inconvenient: difficult or annoying

invested: gave or lent money to something, such as a
company, in the belief that you would get more money
back in the future

launched: started or introduced

manure: the waste that animals leave behind

menagerie (muh **naj** ur ee): a collection of wild or exotic
animals put on display for an audience

outrider: a circus employee on horseback who rode ahead
of the circus

overland: over, by, or through land, rather than by train or
by boat

Percheron (**per** chuh ron) **horse:** a breed of powerful,
rugged work horse from France

portable: able to be moved

provision: supplies of food and drinks

profit: money left over after expenses are subtracted from
money made

pulley: wheel with a groove on the outside in which a
chain or rope can run, used to lift heavy objects

reimburse: to pay someone back the money he or she
spent or lost

secondhand: owned by another person first, used

secure: to keep safe or well protected, to hold

spectacle (**spek** tuh kul): a remarkable or dramatic sight

spectator: person who watches an event but do not take part in it

stock: cattle, sheep, pigs, and other animals typically used on a ranch or farm

suspicious (sus **pih** shus): mistrustful or fearful of something or someone

troupe (troop): a group of performers

water buffalo: a black buffalo found in Asia with long curved horns

wintered: kept, fed, or managed during the winter

yak: a type of ox from central Asia with long, dark shaggy hair

zebu (**zee** boo): a type of ox from India with a large hump over the shoulders

Reading Group Guide and Activities

Discussion Questions

❧ It takes a lot of planning and imagination to run a circus. Take a look at the biographies of the brothers in Chapter 5. What particular skill did each brother have that made their dream of starting a circus possible? Think about your own skills and talents. If you were part of the Ringling family, what part would you play?

❧ To build the world's greatest circus, the Ringling boys had to work together. Without cooperation, the circus never would have been a success. Look back over the story, and find 3 places where the boys came together as a team. Why was it important to cooperate at those key places?

❧ Imagine yourself as part of the Ringling Brothers Circus in the year 1895, performing in a new town each day, and traveling the rails at night. What would it be like to be an animal handler? A waiter in the dining tent? A trapeze artist? Someone who puts up posters advertising the circus coming to town?

Activities and Projects

❧ Just like the Ringling boys did over 100 years ago, it's your turn to create a circus. Using everyone in your class, come up with a plan to put on your own big top performance. You will have to assign roles—clowns, acrobats, and of course a ringmaster. Who is good at handling money? Who might create an ad? Who could keep everyone on track behind the scenes? Who would be good at doing the many jobs that needed to get done, like putting up and taking down the tents? Feeding the animals? Keeping all the costumes clean and ready to go?

❧ Al Ringling and his brothers were what we call **entrepreneurs** (ahn truh preh **nurz**), people who start their own business from scratch. Think of someone you know who started a company or opened his or her own shop or business, and invite that person to visit your class. Before the visit, create a list of interview questions to find out how your guest got started, and what challenges he or she had to overcome.

* Create a poster advertising your own circus. What are the main acts? How much does it cost? What animals are on display? The posters on pages 72 and 74 might give you an idea of where to start.

* Imagine you are Al Ringling, the oldest in a family of circus entrepreneurs. Using details from the book, write a short autobiography that tells the story of how you and your brothers started the circus, and how it came to be such a great success.

To Learn More about the Circus

Apps, Jerry. *Ringlingville USA: The Stupendous Story of Seven Siblings and Their Stunning Circus Success.* Madison: Wisconsin Historical Society Press, 2005.

Clement, Herbert and Dominique Jando. *The Great Circus Parade.* Milwaukee: Gareth Stevens Publishers, 1989.

Dahlinger Jr., Fred and Stuart Thayer. *Badger State Showmen: A History of Wisconsin's Circus Heritage.* Madison: Grote Publishers, 1998.

Downs, Mike. *You See a Circus. I See. . . .* Watertown, MA: Charlesbridge, 2005.

Duncan, Lois. *The Circus Comes Home: When the Greatest Show on Earth Rode the Rails.* New York: Doubleday Books, for Young Readers, 1993.

Elya, Susan Middleton. *Say Hola to Spanish at the Circus.* New York: Lee & Low Books, 2000.

Gaskin, Carol and John Klein. *A Day in the Life of a Circus Clown.* Mahwah, NJ: Troll Associates, 1988.

Granfield, Linda. *Circus: An Album*. New York: DK
Publishing, 1998.

Horner, William. *Snyder and Baldy: Wisconsin Circus
Elephants*. Green Bay: Badger House, 2001.

Janeczko, Paul B. *Worlds Afire*. Cambridge, MA: Candlewick
Press, 2004.

McClung, Robert. *Old Bet and the Start of the American
Circus*. New York: Morrow Junior Books, 1993.

Presnall, Judith Janda. *Circuses: Under the Big Top*. New York:
Franklin Watts, 1996.

Sís, Peter. *The Train of States*. New York: Greenwillow Books,
2004.

Sloan, Mark. *Wild, Weird, and Wonderful: The American
Circus 1901–1927 as Seen by F.W. Glasier*. New York:
The Quantuck Lane Press, 2003.

Weil, Lisl. *Let's Go to the Circus*. New York: Holiday House,
1988.

Acknowledgments

Fred Dahlinger Jr., former Director of Historic Resources and Facilities at Circus World Museum in Baraboo, Wisconsin, convinced me to write a history of the Ringling brothers and their famous circus. He pointed me toward much of the research that led to the publication of *Ringlingville USA*, the version of this book for adult readers.

Along the way, many others helped. The list includes circus historians Fred D. Pfening III, his father Fred D. Pfening Jr., Richard J. Reynolds III, and Stuart LeR. Thayer. Paul Ringling, the grandson of Alf T. Ringling, one of the 5 brothers, was of special help in sorting out the Ringling history. Sara Phillips, Wisconsin Historical Society Press Editor, deserves special mention for helping to make this book readable for young people.

For this children's book, my daughter Susan Apps Horman, who is a reading teacher at Sherman Middle School in Madison, read the entire manuscript several times and offered many suggestions for improvement. Thanks also to my son Steve, staff photographer for the *Wisconsin State Journal*, who took the contemporary photos for the book. And not to be forgotten is my wife Ruth, who reads all of my work, draft after draft, searching for errors and suggesting what to take out and what to add.

Bobbie Malone, Director of the Office of School Services for the Wisconsin Historical Society deserves special praise for developing this biography series. What better way to learn about Wisconsin history than to read the stories of the people who made this state what it is.

Index

This index points you to the pages where you can read about persons, places, and ideas. If you do not find the word you are looking for, try to think of another word that means about the same thing.

When you see a page number in **bold** it means there is a picture or a map on that page.

A

accidents, 23
acrobats, 20, 31
admission prices, 6-7, 10, 15, 23, 49
advance man, 17, 19, 21, 38
advertising
  circus, 7-8, **12**, 59-61, 64, **65**, 85, 94,95
  hall shows, **11, 19**
  handbills, **30**
  magazines, 20
  newspapers, 59-60, 85, 94-95
  posters, **23, 33, 55**, 60-61, **62, 72, 74, 86, 90**
aerialists, 51
Al Ringling Theater, 57, **58**

alligators, 5
animals, 5, 7-8
  care in winter, 29, 80-81
  food, 38
  health of, 78
  training, 31, 77, **83–84**, 83-85
antelopes, 70
audiences, 15, 23, 35

B

bands, 24, 48, **48**, 49, 60, 62
Baraboo, Wisconsin, 12, 22, 25, **28**, 29, 35, 57, 79-80, 86, 88
baritone, 62, **62**
barbershop, **35**

bareback riders, 51, **76**
bears, 5
Bridgeport, Connecticut, 89
Brodhead, Wisconsin, 9-10

C
camels, 31, 33, 70, **78**
candy stand, **40**, 49-50
Circus World Museum, 86
circus routes, 28-29, 34
circuses
  Barnum & Bailey Circus, 89-90, **90**
  Dan Rice's Riverboat Circus, 5
  Parson and Roy's Great
    Palace Show, 12
  penny circus, 6-9
  riverboat circus, 5-6
  clowns, 5, 31, 48, **51**, 52
  cooking, 39, 43-44
  cornet, 17, **17**
  costumes, 85, **87**

D
dancers, 31
deer, 31, 33, 70
dogs, 7, 70, 77, **77**

E
elephants, **21**, 31, 33, **43**, 72-73, **73**, 88
  as workers, 45-46, 70
  as performers, 5, 48, 51, 70-71, **72**,
  83, **83**
  baby, **72**, 73
  employees, 25, 27, 31, 56, 64, 68, 81-83

F
factories, 4
food, 38, 43-44, **44**

G
giraffes, 70, **70**
gnus, 70

H
hall shows, 11, 13-15, 17, 19
  first, 14-18
  map, **16**
  number of shows, 18, 20
  routes, **16**, 16-17
  travel, 11, 15, 17
hippopotamus, 33, 70, 74, **74**
honesty, 18, 56, 59
horses, 29, 31, 33
  harnesses, 3-4, 10, 12-13
  performing, 5-6, 48, **48**, 70, **76, 77, 84**,
  84-85
  working, **3, 41**, 41-42, **42**, 45-46, 76, 88

I
ibexes, 70

J
jugglers, 8-9, 13, 24, 51, 57

K
kangaroos, 31, 70

L
lions, 31, 48, 70

M

Mazomanie, Wisconsin, 14-15
McGregor, Iowa, **1**, 1-2, **2**
menagerie, 31, 33, **69**, 69-78
money, 10-11, 14, 58-59, 86, 94
expenses, 15, 55
  house, 15
  income, 15, 20, 30, 55
  profits, 31, 55
monkeys, 5, 31, 33
music, 5, 11, 17, 52
musical instruments, 13, **13**, **17**, 17-18,
  62, **62**

O

ostriches, 5
outrider, 26

P

parades, **6**, 6-7, 17, 48, **48**, 51, 86-87, **87**
performers, **4**, 5, 14, **20**, **24**, 48, **52**, 63, 82
  acrobats, 20, 31
  aerialists, 51
  bareback riders, 51, **76**
  clowns, 5, 31, 48, **51**, 52
  contortionists, 20
  dancers, 31
  gymnasts, 20
  jugglers, 8-9, 13, 24, 51, 57
  sideshow, 49, **49**
performances
  first circus, 6-9
  in barns, 8
  music, 5, 11, 17, 52
  number of, 29
post office, **36**

R

rhinoceros, 70, 74-75, **75**
Rice, Dan, 5
Ringling, Albert, "Al," 2-3, 6, 9-14, 19, **55**,
  55-58, **56** , 77, **93**, 93-94
Ringling, Alfred Theodore, "Alf T.," 2-3,
  12-15, 19, 55, **55**, **59**, 59-60, 89, **93**,
  94-95
Ringling, August, 3, 12, **93**
Ringling, Augustus, "Gus," 2-3, 12, 55, **55**,
  64, **64**, **93**, 94
Ringling, Carl, "Charles," 2-3, 12-13, 19,
  55, **55**, 60-62, **61**, 89, **93**, 95
Ringling, Henry, 2, 12, 31, 55, **55**, 65, **65**,
  93, 95-96
Ringling, Ida, 12, 91, **93**
Ringling, John, 2-3, 12-13, 19, 55, **55**,
  63, 63-64, 89-91, **93**, 95
Ringling, Lou, **34**
Ringling, Salome, 7, 13, **93**
Ringling, William, "Otto," 2-3, 12, 19, 55,
  55, 58-59, **59**, **93**, 94
Ringling brothers
  as partners, 18-20, 28-29, 31, 54-56,
  65-67
  as performers, 6, 8-10, 13, 24, 60, 62
Ringlingville, 33-34, **35**, **37**, 47
ringmaster, 50, 56
riverboat, 1, 4-6
Robinson, "Yankee," **22**, 22-23, 27

S

sideshow, 49, **49**
snakes, 33, **34**, 70

T

tents, 41, **45**
  big top, 22-23, 41, 45, 50, **50**, 53, **66, 67**
  boss canvasman, 43, 53
  buying, 14, 20
  packing, 25-26
  poles, 22, 44, 46, **46**
  putting up, 22, 43, 45-46, **46, 47**
  stakes, 22, 45, **45**
taking down, 25, 53-54
tigers, **v**, 5, 70
tightrope walker, 8-9, 24
timeline, 97-99
trains, **32**, 32-33, 42, 63, **65**
  loading and unloading, 36-39, 41-43,
  53-54, 80, **87**
trapeze artists, 51
travel, 13, 25-26, **26**, 30, 32, 34, 95
trumpet, 13
tuba, 13

V

violin, 13, **13**, 17

W

wagons
  circus, **32, 47**, 48, 88
  equipment, 21, 25-27, 32, 40-41, 44,
  53, 70
water buffalo, 33, 70
weather, 17, 26-27, 30
winter quarters, 78-88, **79, 80, 88**
  equipment storage, 29, 81
wolves, 33, 70

Z

zebras, 33, 70, **71**, 88, **88**
zebu, 31, 33